To Fall In Love

Emeli Dion

Copyright© 2021 Emeli Dion
ISBN: 978-81-8253-806-1

First Edition: 2021
Rs. 200/-

Cyberwit.net
HIG 45 Kaushambi Kunj, Kalindipuram
Allahabad - 211011 (U.P.) India
http://www.cyberwit.net
Tel: +(91) 9415091004
E-mail: info@cyberwit.net

No part of this book may be reproduced or transmitted in any form or by
any means, electronic, mechanical, photocopying, or otherwise, without
the express written consent of Emeli Dion.

Printed at VCORE LLP.

Contents

To Find a Home

To find a home in someone
Is a rare and beautiful thing.
I was lucky.
I was lucky enough to find a home in you.

So often was I neglected and abandoned
By those who I held dear to my heart.
But you? You stayed through the storm
And could outrun the weather.
You saw my broken pieces
As a worn-down whole.

You were the one to see past the gleam in my eyes
And unmask the dark interior that I had held myself
Hostage in for so long.
And I could do the same for you.

Our dark and injured souls came together in the stars
And burst with a light so bright
That no eyes could bear to see it.
Our minds and bodies became one unit
In the midst of our darkest days,
When we felt shattered.

I built a shelter in the love you gave me,
Hiding from the past.
You kept a fire burning in my heart
Where it had been cold for many years.

Here, I was safe.
With you, I knew I could stop running
From all that had hurt me.
And you felt the same.
We planted a garden of security to ward off
The knots we had so often felt trapped in our chests.

The pit in our stomachs had been full
Of a tangled mess,
But we unraveled all that was woven
And tasted serenity for the first time.

Yes, to find a home in someone
Is not simple or always possible.
But if one is lucky enough to do so,
Then they will forever feel as light as a cloud
As their thoughts and dreams are calmed
By a wave of irenic contentment.

Floating

Have you ever felt like you were floating?
Like the air you were breathing was helium,
Filling you up like a balloon?
I know I have.
I met you and my lungs were immediately filled
With a breath so light and so beautiful
That I thought I might stop breathing altogether.
My heart started to beat faster,
The butterflies in my stomach waking from their slumber.
When I met you, I finally felt alive again.
My nerves sent electricity through my entire body,
And my knees nearly buckled.
But your laugh kept me up.
I stared into your eyes and thought I could see a galaxy,
Waiting to bring me to a brand new planet.
You quickly became what kept me going.

All That Is Silent

After being denied my own voice and opinion for so long,
I gave up trying to speak.
But that didn't matter to you.
I was tired and worn,
And wanted nothing more than to be understood.
You understood who I am because
You too knew what it was like to stay silent.
Our silence rang through the night
As our presence under the moonlight spoke
More powerfully than any words could.

It was astonishingly beautiful to read
Someone's story without saying a single thing.

We were both broken and hurt,
But that didn't stop us from living.

If we didn't have anyone else,
We at least had each other.
So many people forgot that we were suffering
Because we stayed quiet and braved through
All that haunted us.
Our eyes were heavy with tears that forgot to fall,
But we had finally found something that didn't
Drown us in the ocean of pain and lies.
We found a love that would fill the ocean with
Fire so fierce that no pain could survive.

Saving

For a time longer than I cared to remember,
I had wished for someone to understand me better than I could.
I wanted someone to save me
Because I knew deep down that I couldn't save myself.

I wanted to be taken care of the way I cared for others.
I wanted someone to bring the sides out of me
That I thought were long gone.
Then, we met and my entire world shifted.
You were the one to make the sun shine
While I was stuck in the rain.

You lit up the dark tunnel I was hiding in.
I had always wanted to find a person who would tell me
It was okay to not feel completely alright all the time;
To validate that what I was feeling was real.

You were my savior in the rough sea
Of my pain and suffering.
I finally found someone who cared enough
To stay with me through all that was bad
Until I could find the good in life again.
But even then you stayed.

We indulged in the happiness we built.
We didn't have to be afraid anymore.

Stormy Seas

In the midst of the storm,
You made me calm.
The feelings of anger and sadness
Were no longer trapped in my chest.
A peaceful wave came crashing down
And washed out all that was bad.
The sea of negativity finally found a way to rest.
You were the one positive thing
That kept me from drowning.
So often had I wished to hold on to an anchor
And sink down to the bottom of the ocean.
But now, I stayed perched on a life raft,
Trying to find my way home.
I was lost, yes.
But you were my compass.
You became my home.
Despite the terrors of the dark water below,
I found a light shining bright in you
That I could look to when I was afraid.
That fear had once consumed me,
But you freed me from its shackles.
I could finally find peace
In one of the most chaotic of places
With you by my side.

Flowered Knife

Many people always chose to hand me a knife
And expected me to use it against myself.
So when you handed me a flower,
I knew not what to do.
I could smell its sweet fragrance
As it blew through the breeze.
It whispered kind words to me
And I found myself in a field of tall grass,
The sunlight resting upon my skin.
You had a smile on your face
That made me feel at rest.
In a world so full of chaos,
That moment felt as calm as a stream in the woods.
I had often looked at the world
With hatred and animosity,
Even in this vast field.
But you changed that.
I could now find beauty in all that I disliked,
Even in the most ugly of things.
When given a knife, you can only see its violence.
But if you give me a flower,
I can finally see splendor in all that surrounds me.

Stay

When people came into my life before I met you,
I so desperately wanted to ask them to stay
Because I knew they too would leave like others.
No matter how hard I tried to keep them around,
They always left.
I gave them all I had left in me.
When you showed up,
I had nothing left.
But that was okay.
You had so much to offer and I was afraid to take it.
But you gave me happiness, security, and love,
All wrapped up with a bow.
It seemed too perfect, so unreal.
But it wasn't.
And for the first time in my life,
I didn't feel like I had to beg someone to stay,
To not leave me behind in the dust.
You refused to abandon me.

New Light

On Sunday mornings, I would wake up
And look out the window to see gray clouds
Rolling across the sky.
I would drink black coffee while reading the same old news.
I would read books in the afternoons
That I had already read a hundred times before.
I would sit in the same rocking chair on my porch.
The flowers in my garden were no longer full of color.
That all changed, though, when you moved in.
Suddenly, on Sunday mornings,
I would wake up to a bright sun
Shining through that same window.
I made my coffee taste a little sweeter
And I didn't have to read the paper anymore
Or those old and dusty books.
No, instead I could watch you dance around the kitchen,
Playing music and making pancakes.
That rocking chair now had a fresh layer of paint
And it rocked better than ever.
Together, we fixed the garden I had let go.
It now bloomed with all colors.
My world had changed forever
And my heart felt much lighter.
Finally, I had found my light.
It was you all along.

Broken Pieces

My heart had been ripped in half,
Then broken into pieces by people I once loved
It was battered and tired.
My lungs could no longer hold much air
And my mind was empty.
I was but a shell of what I once tried to be;
But all I felt was hurt and in pain.
So much of my once bright and wonderful world
Was now dark and cold.
Rain washed away more and more of me each day,
Until you came with an umbrella to keep me dry.
First, you kept me safe from the rain.
But then you protected me from all that caused pain.
You picked up the pieces of my heart
And made it whole again.
You filled my lungs back up with air
And let lovely thoughts flood into my mind.
The days became filled with light
And I finally felt warmth.

Forever In Love

Many people said that our love wouldn't last forever.
They said we were too young to know what love was.
But we weren't.
Love was all we had in our lives.
We were neglected and beat down
By everyone but each other.
Our eyes held sadness,
But they were still bright.
So we didn't let people ruin what we had.
And now, I can say with all the confidence in the world
That I'll still love you when we're old and gray,
Our faces covered with wrinkles.
Our eyes will still be bright
And our hearts will continue to burn
With a fiery passion that nobody was able to put out.
My love, I'll adore you forever and ever,
With not a single soul capable of stopping me.

Fearful

A small part of me has always been afraid of love.
The commitment, the fear of losing the one,
The complications.

I used to worry that I wasn't capable of being loved,
That I was unlovable and didn't deserve what I now have.
Despite the fears, though, I have found
That this feeling you give me is the most beautiful thing
I have ever experienced.

Sure, we face challenges and find hills to climb,
But at the end of the day,
I wouldn't trade this for the world.

For the first time, I am no longer afraid.
With you by my side, giving me all I rejected in the past,
I feel okay.
My thoughts have been calmed,
My racing heart no longer beating as fast.

I can sleep better at night as I think of sweet things,
My dreams furnished with images of you.

Blank Pages

My poetry would often feel like a lump in your throat,
The words getting stuck as I choked out
What I was feeling.
They wouldn't flow like a river onto the page,
Rather they slowly appeared,
Like the tears that used to fall onto my cheeks.
I would stare at the blank sheet in front of me
And wonder how it was possible to write anything
When I felt so empty.
But now?
My poetry is like a love song,
With the most beautiful of harmonies.
The words I had so much trouble finding before
Now flood into my mind
Like a waterfall that's eager to reach the stream below.
The blank pages I was once so intimidated by
Are full of ink.
My heart races as I write line upon line,
And the empty pit inside of me
Has been filled with love and warmth.

Something Real

I was never a real fan of people.
I had been abused and hurt one time too many,
So finding someone like you was never a thought.
I put myself out there again and again
Only to face the same results.
I had forgotten that not all people are terrible.
I had forgotten that some people know love
And are capable of sharing it.
At first, I was hesitant to let you in.
But now that I have, I found my way to love once more.
My hope had long ago been shattered
By selfish egos and fake personalities.
To find someone genuine was nearly an aspiration
That even the most experienced dreamers
Had trouble achieving.
It appears, despite being hopeless and refusing to dream,
That even I could find my person.
Because really, out of all the people in the world,
You are the only one I'll ever want.

Heartless Leaving

I fell so deeply, so hard, so quick.
I was happy and content, but sadly you were not.
You pretended that I mattered,
You made me feel alive.
Then you left and took it all away,
Saying our love had died.
But was it ever there to start?
On your end, that is.
I knew what I felt was real,
But what you claimed to feel was simply a mirage.
You made me believe that you loved me back,
That you were what I needed.
You kept me going every day,
Until I was broken hearted.
Turns out that a liar is never a good enough reason.
So now I live with regret and pain,
But my heart is still full of love.
Now that you're gone I've found another reason,
But it's someone who cares for my heart.

Replaced

As I looked at the stars in the night sky,
I couldn't help but notice how dull they appeared to be.
Many things that emit light became dull
The very moment I met you.
You became the brightest light I've ever seen.
You radiated positivity and warmth
That not even the sun could provide.

You even put the moon's beauty to shame.
Flowers no longer smelled as sweet
And even the grass ceased to look as green
As it once did.
All the things I found to be beautiful,
All the things I once held near to my heart
Were replaced by images of you.

My simple cup of coffee every day
Turned into kissing you each morning.

Taking a walk through the forest alone
Became our Sunday afternoon cuddles
While we watched our favorite movies.
Everything I once loved came together harmoniously
Into human form.
The feelings I got from doing my favorite things
Could only arise if I was with you.

Whether it was staring into your eyes
Or holding your hand.

Or it was hearing your heartbeat as I laid my head
On your chest while the small intimate moments
That so many people looked over
Became what I loved the most.
You became what I loved most.

Shadows of Light

When I showed you all of the darkness within me,
You decided to stay.
You didn't step back in fear
Or treat me any different.
You looked me in the eyes with a smile
And told me it was alright.
You shared your deepest secrets with me
And we basked in the fact that we weren't alone.
We had both been trapped in our own minds
With no one else to go to.
Everyone else was afraid of the darkness
Because it would block the light they once saw in us.
Despite the shadows we cast,
Together we were able to form our own light.

Addicted

Loving you is an intoxicating feeling.
No matter how hard I try to stop,
I simply cannot.
Some people become addicted to alcohol,
Others prefer drugs.
My only addiction is you.
I can feel the withdrawals when you are not near.
My heart feels heavy, my mind scattered.
But when you come back,
I gain all of my senses back
Like a gust of wind.
The very feeling itself nearly knocks me over.
I get a tightness in my chest,
As if the love is so alluring that it aches.
My love, I am drawn to you.
I am captured by your flaws,
Fascinated by your perfections.
All of your pieces have come together in my heart
As a whole, shocking me to life again and again.
Each time I think that I cannot love you more,
You give me reason to.
Of all the sensations one can experience in life,
This one is by far my favorite.

A Place Unseen

In the place you put me in your heart,
I found a world unseen by even the dark.
It was cold and unforgivable.
I couldn't see or hear a single thing.
The only thing I felt was my heart beating.
I lit a fire with a single match,
That soon lit the space up.
And there I found all that was lost,
All that you had desired.
There were cracks and holes,
The floor boards no longer sturdy.
So I patched it up
And made you feel worthy.
You had long ago forgotten
What it was like to be loved.
I filled your heart up once more
So that you too could be engulfed
By a wave of love so strong
And so powerful that nobody could
Take it from you again.
I discovered your passion, your fire, your anger.
I took it all in and climbed up the ladder.
Together we defeated the demons you held.
We found hope in each other
And saved one another.

When, You...

When my heart stopped beating,
You brought me back to life.
When my lungs stopped breathing,
You filled me up with air.
When my brain stopped trying,
You pushed me to go on.

When I found it hard to stay awake,
You let me use your lap as a pillow.
When I didn't want to eat,
You brought me my favorite food.
When I didn't want to stay,
You gave me reasons to.

When I found hope again,
You gave me a smile.
When I smiled back,
You cried a little.
When I admitted my love,
You said you loved me back.

From a place so dark,
To finding a place of light.
You were there for the bad,
Knowing you'd find something good.

Genre: Romance

Music used to have simple melodies.
The lyrics in love songs were the same
In everything I heard.
The chorus was another sappy story.

Books used to be drawn out sentences.
The middle of the story was the same turn of events.
The ending was just another happy one
That many longed to find.

Movies had the same plot with different characters.
The kissing in the rain scene became overrated.
That one moment when you could see a shift
In characters was a look all too familiar.

Suddenly, I had my own plot twist.

Music now had intricate harmonies
That made me feel like floating.
The lyrics quickly applied to my every feeling.
The choruses made me light up each time I heard them.

Books became full of beautiful chapters.
The middle of the story now brought
Happy tears to my eyes.
The ending left me wanting to read more.

The romantic plot in all of those movies
Was now the dream I was living.

Anytime I was kissed, I hoped it would be in the rain.
My shift was when I saw my love's eyes.

When I fell in love, my entire view of romance
Shifted into a world of understanding.

Petals, Thorns, Roots

I like to picture myself as a rose.
Before you, everyone fell in love with my
Deep red petals.
But once the colder times came,
They forgot that I was more than a flower.
As the petals fell, and the leaves started to wilt,
They neglected to remember my roots.
They feared my thorns.
But you didn't.
You took hold of the stem, of my broken pieces,
And held me close.
You recognized my roots, my past,
And didn't forget that the pain of my past existed.
You knew that even when my petals were gone,
I was still alive.
Flowers are so often seen as beautiful
Until they lose their color.
But is the flower dead? No.
It lives on until it can form its petals again.
Even when I'm in my darkest hours,
You are the one to help me find my light.

Ache For My Soul

We stood under the night sky
In a silence so strong that we could
Hear the stars whispering to each other.
The moon was casting a light
Just bright enough so we could see one another.
Just before our silence rang through
The vast field we stood in,
We expressed our desire to find someone
Who would ache for our very souls.
Though our souls held pain and trauma
Unknown to anyone else,
We still hoped to find the one person
Who would crave it still.
But as I stood, avoiding eye contact
And searching for the right things to say,
It hit me.
I wanted you to ache for my soul.
I wanted you to be the one who held me close
And loved me for the mess I was.
I turned to looka at you and our eyes finally met.
That very moment, the silence we had found
To be awkward became louder and more powerful
Than our unspoken words could ever be.
One look and I knew we felt the same thing.
It was like a magnet pulling our souls closer together.
One look and I knew that we were
The ones for each other.
We said nothing, but even the stars and the moon
Could sense the connection we formed
In such a simple moment.

Describe a Love

Honey coffee, fresh lilacs,
Old books, and light rain.
Swollen lips, bright eyes,
Beating hearts, and heavy breathing.

Rolling clouds, mowed grass,
Running streams, and new growth.
Holding hands, watching movies,
Bedtime cuddles, and soft gazes.

Loud thunder, colorful sunsets,
Finding passion, and loving others.
Sharing moments, being honest,
Deep talks, and sharing secrets.

Taking pictures, appreciating life,
Wonderful experiences, and finding art.
Endless communication, grand gestures,
Sarcastic humor, and speaking kindly.

To describe a love
Is hard to do simply.
But for my love,
The words all come easily.

My Muse

Every artist finds their muse.
A lover, nature, perhaps someone dear to them.
All of these pages filled with ink
Spill the intricacies of how I feel
When I think of you.
You are my muse.
You inspire me to write.

You inspire me to live.
Every small moment we all,
All of the secrets we share,
Lead my hand to write the words
That my poetry displays.
To speak such words would leave me
Never wanting to speak again.

But I cannot leave them unsaid,
So I write them instead.
These pages leave space for me to unwrap
All I wish to say to you,
With just enough room left for interpretation.
My lines cross the line between what is to be said
And what many choose to leave unspoken.

Fear itself inhibits so many minds
From expressing why something
Or someone is their muse.
But my mind does not fear my love for you.
My mind embraces it so fully
That it can't bear to keep it hidden away.
It simply cannot bear to hide its muse.

Destinations

When I tried to follow a map,
With no determined destination,
I led myself to you.
Even when I was passing by unfamiliar sights,
My heart told me to keep going.
The road was long, and I was becoming weary.
But I couldn't stop my journey.
I was alone and scared,
And wondered if I'd find what I was looking for.
When our eyes first met, I knew to stop.
After searching for so long,
With roads unseen by even the most detailed maps,
I had found you.
The connection was so instant
That I thought I could see sparks fly.
I knew nothing about you, not even your name,
But I felt safe in your gaze.
Our encounter was very brief,
And we soon parted our ways.
But I knew one day we'd find each other once more
And experience this delight all over again.

My Hometown

I decided to take you to my hometown.

It was full of old buildings, cows, and fields.

I took you to all of my favorite places,

Even ones I kept a secret.

We had homemade jam and tasty pizza.

We saw horses on the road,

And dogs in yards.

It wasn't much, but you loved every second.

When I saw your face light up,

I knew that you were the one.

I had warned you that there wasn't much to do,

And that my mom might ask you too many questions.

But you enjoyed everything.

I brought you to the house I grew up in

And showed you my room.

I thought you might laugh at my old stuffed bear,

Or my small knickknacks,

But you stared at them in awe.

My dad stayed quiet,

But had a look of approval when he saw you.

Though my hometown might not be much,

Having you in it makes it feel like something more.

Learn To Forgive

When you unveiled the terrible things
You had gone through in an attempt
To push me away,
I revealed a never-ending love.

You were scared to have found someone
Who accepted you for all you were.
The understanding came easy to me.
I too had endured things that hurt
And I used that to push away those I cared about.

So I took our hurt and turned it
Into an unbreakable bond.
We had both gone through dark times all alone
So now we had no choice but to pretend
That we weren't desperate for help from others.
But together, slowly but surely,
We found comfort in knowing each other's pain.

Together, we were able to heal some of the wounds
That had been cut so deeply into our being
That we could barely distinguish who we once were
From who we had become.

We learned to forgive ourselves for all that
Happened to us and we forgave ourselves
For all that we could not be.
Our terrible pasts merged together
And we finally learned how to love.

Slow Dance

I never liked to dance,
But when you put that record on and grabbed my waist,
My feet became eager to move.
In the dimmed living room, the couch pushed back,
We moved together as one,
Our bodies flowing as smooth as a river.
We were dressed in sweatpants and t-shirts,
But it didn't matter.
Our socks helped us glide across that floor
So well that it felt like we were on ice.
We spun in circles, forgetting time existed.
When the song ended, after what felt like eternity,
We stopped to catch our breaths.
I looked into your eyes
And couldn't help but smile.
After that night, I wanted to dance again and again.
On certain nights while we made dinner,
We'd slow dance as we waited.
At parties, we would take over the dance floor
And dance until our feet hurt.
I really didn't like to dance
But as long as it was with you,
I would keep spinning until my last day.

Life Isn't Always Beautiful

Life isn't always beautiful.
But our love is something that will
Never cease to be beautiful.
Despite our flaws,
Despite all we encounter,
The love we share will always amaze me.
In life, we will face dark times
That will haunt our dreams.
We will face things unimaginable
That will make us question if life's worth it.
But in the end, as long as we have each other,
There really is no other life that I'd want to live.
How can I be fearful of what's to happen
When there are flowers blooming,
The sun shining, and you by my side?
So much is unknown.
So much remains to be unseen.
But I do know this:
My love for you will forever burn brightly,
As we find all that does make life beautiful.

All I Have Left

Though I may be broken in some places,
I promise to love you
With every piece left in me.

I will continue to love you,
Even if there is nothing left.
Once I have nothing,
I will pick myself back up again and again
So I can continue to love you.

I will pick myself apart and search
For anything that will fill me back up.
But even when I reach rock bottom,
I know that I may not have to keep searching.

I know, in the depths of my heart,
That you will be there for me
Through all I experience.

You know in your heart that I will love you
No matter what and you'll love me too.
Broken or not, what we share
As two people together cannot be defeated
By what is thrown our way.

The world can try to tear us apart
But we will always be able to put each other

Back together again.
My love, we will never fall.

We are going to find all the strength
Left in us and become unstoppable.

Work Of Art

There are so many expectations
That people have for you.
But me?
I don't have to expect anything from you.
My dear, you are art.
You make me feel so many things
Just by seeing you.
You have so much soul,
And a beautiful one in fact.
Art can cause confusion,
But I only find clarity when I look at you.
Though so many people see you as a thunderstorm,
I can only see you as the shining sun
That others are searching for.
Your lovers before me found you easy to replace.
But to me, you are irreplaceable.
There's not a single person I have met
To be as glorious and incredible as you are.
In my eyes, you put even the most
Famous people to shame.
I would say that you are like my favorite celebrity,
But really I'd rather compare you
To my favorite painting.
Celebrities come and go.
But a painting is more permanent.
And I want you to stay much longer.
You have a positivity in you
That radiates and I never want to lose that.
I never want to lose you.

Dark Paths

As I tried so desperately to get lost
On the path I was supposed to follow,
You led me in another direction.
I wanted to disappear, to disappoint.
I wanted to lose myself
To the demons that haunted the trail I was on.

But you knew that all I really
Wanted was to be saved.
You saw past the mask I wore
To protect myself from others.

You were able to see and understand
My fragmented interior.
So you dragged me through all
That troubled me to reach
The other side of my unhealed trauma.
I wanted to fight back, to tell you to stop.

But I couldn't.
I let you take hold of me.
I finally accepted your help
And was able to love myself.

I fell in love with you too.
You were the first person to let me be myself.
You forced me to face what many people
Thought to be fake.
You made me face the darkness that had been
Tearing me down for so many years.

I finally had a foundation
To build off of
And I had you to be there along the way.
I finally found someone who cared.

I Do

When I asked you one question,
And you responded with one word,
Our lives changed forever.
Only five words total were exchanged
In that moment, but our emotions
And feelings spoke more than we
Were capable of doing.
The gleam in our eyes, the smiles on our lips,
And the butterflies in our stomachs
Let the universe know that we were
To be bonded and intertwined
By our very souls for eternity.
A lot of people were afraid of that word: eternity.
It means forever, and forever never seemed
To be such a likely promise.
But we weren't afraid.
We made a commitment to each other,
To our love.
It made us giddy.
It made me want to dance.
And so we did.
The best night of our lives, after we said I do,
We danced until the moon stopped shining
And the sun came out of hiding.
After that night, our love tied its knot,
Never to be destroyed.
And it never was.

Earth's Memory

The ancient life within
These trees has a memory.
So I often wonder,
Will the trees remember us?
Will they remember our story and
Whisper it to other young lovers?
Will they take our tragic backstory and teach
People that love can come from
The most unlikely of places?
Will the running river nearby
Hear our nervous hearts beating and
Remind those who pass by what it feels like
When you're with someone who
Gives you butterflies?
I wonder to myself if the leaves on the forest floor
Will remember our soft footsteps
As we drew closer together.
I think back to the small plants,
Just beginning their lives.
Will those plants grow knowing
That you can be young and still be powerful,
Just as we were?
My love, I know I'll always remember
Our love story.
But will the rest of the world?

Destroy

I've forever been cautious enough
To not let anyone destroy me.
Yes, I have been damaged many times before,
But never have I been destroyed.
But here is the problem.
I met you and instantly I thought to myself
That you could ruin me.
But that is not the issue.
The fact is, I would let you destroy me.

I would let you put your hands around my throat
While you looked into my eyes with that sparkle
And took everything away from me.
I would be too overcome with love and joy.
I would look at the few inches between us
And feel lucky enough to simply be close to you.
Dear, I have never loved anyone so much
That I would allow them to ultimately end me.
There is no fear within me, though.

I know that no matter what,
You will not choose to hurt me in that way.
Our emotions have flowed together in a stream
That gently trickles through the world.
We are in tune with each other
And can understand one another
On a level that nobody can imagine.
It's as though we have become one person,
Soaring under the stars, waiting for our moment.

Perspective

I am someone different
To all the people I know.
To some I'm sweet.
To others I'm quiet.
A few think I'm funny,
While some don't know me at all.

But I often wondered,
Who am I?
I have rarely been able to distinguish
Who I think I am compared to
How other people view me.

I wracked my mind trying to figure out
How I truly view myself.

Your view has always been pleasant.
I thought you were exaggerating it
Or perhaps trying to make me feel better.
But you weren't.
In times when I felt most unidentified
By my own senses,
You showed me who I am.
You didn't say that I was kind,
You didn't say that I was pretty.

You showed me what I did for others
And how it made a positive impact.

You took a mirror and cracked the glass,
Then told me I didn't need it anyway.
You were patient when I said
I didn't believe you and took the time
To show me it all over again.

You loved me and you wanted me to love myself.
You saw so many things in me
That I could never see
And you made sure that I would
One day see myself through your eyes.
And I finally did.

Just A Warning

Your mother warned you about
A certain type of person.
She told you to stay away from
The ones who are reckless and cold.

You had encountered that type before
And you were afraid when you met me.
But that's not who I am.
I will hold you close when you've had a bad day.
I'll dry your tears when you cry at night.

I'll stand by your side even when
You try to push me away.
Because even when it feel like
You love me less,
Or you've decided you're better off alone,
I'll love you still.

My heart is constantly full of love to give,
Despite rarely receiving such love back.
I too have encountered people
Who only want to break you,
But what choice do I have other than to move on?
And so I'll help you too.

I'll teach you about the wonders of romance.
I'll kiss you when you're sad,
Pick you up when you're feeling down.

I'll put aside all of the baggage I carry
Just to help carry yours.

This may make you skeptical,
To have met someone who cares so much.
But believe me, there's nothing unreal about it.
I'm yours forever, as long as you want me.

Bad Days

Some days I would feel as though
I could win my battles.

There would be days when I thought
I could make it.
But then there were days where
I'd cry on the bathroom floor and
Wonder why I couldn't be good enough.
I'd lay in my bed at night and
Stare at the ceiling, feeling completely numb.
There was no consistency in my life.

I was waiting, hoping to find someone
Who could pick me up off the floor and
Tell me it was okay.
You were the one to become my constant.
No matter how many times I told myself
That I wasn't a good person,
No matter how often I would
Put myself down,
You always threw positivity in my face.

You forced me to see that I was enough,
That things would be okay, even when they weren't.
Even when I was sitting on the floor,
Questioning whether I should go or not,
You were by my side the whole time.
Even if you had to drag me through it all,

You made sure I would get out.
My battles became easier, my burdens lighter.

I finally had someone to save me
From myself.

Love Flaws

You once told me to say that I didn't love you
I tried, but it was a lie.
I loved you furiously and completely.

You were afraid to hurt me
Because you had flaws.
So I learned to love every single flaw
Until there were none.
You thought you were toxic.
I took whatever toxicity you believed to exist
And turned it from poison into something beautiful.

I took every little thing you thought
Was wrong with yourself
And made sure that you could see
How wonderful I thought you were.

There were no faults that I could see.
I knew that you were the best thing
I would ever have in my life
And I made it my mission to let you see that too.
Perfection itself is a silly concept,
As nothing will ever be completely perfect,
But you certainly come close to it.

No matter how often you think to be
A horrible person,
I will forever prove you wrong.

Caramel

Caramel light spills into the room,
The morning dew slipping in through the window.
Your delightful scent lingers on the pillow,
And I can't help but smile.
I hear the coffee brewing,
Its strong smell filling the air.
We spend our morning eating breakfast,
Enjoying each other's company.

Despite not doing anything significant,
Our time is well spent.
Simply being in your presence is enough.
I am constantly and inexhaustibly obsessed
With your soul and your heart.
Just seeing you makes my own heart beat faster
As if it has a race to win.
My chest becomes filled with an air
Lighter than anything I've ever felt.

To be able to sit at this table with you
In such early hours makes me feel
Like we are the only two people in the world.
Just you and I and our love,
Together in a small space and appreciating
Every single second.
This is my happy place.
You make me happy.

Deep Conversations

To have an intellectual conversation
With you fills me with joy.
To talk about love, life, everything.
I have such a deep affection for it.
To see your eyes light up when you speak
Of the mysteries of the world
Makes mine light up too.

When we agree on something and have to stop
For a minute to process what we've
Discovered about life,
I think about how alike we are.
There is so much wonder in the way our lives intertwine.
Not everyone is lucky enough
To find someone who acts as
Their other half, but I'm lucky enough to have found you.

When we look up at the stars at night
As we talk or sit in silence,
I can see them align to form our perfect story.
I used to think that it was a coincidence
To have met one another,
But perhaps it's what the universe intended.
No matter what, I am glad
To have found you.

I will forever love you and
The way we understand one another.
I will always love the way we can talk

About the most controversial of topics
And end them with a smile,
Still loving each other.
My, how I love you.

Remember

Remember when you wrote me that letter
So many years ago?
The one with your scratchy handwriting
And a couple of words misspelled.
Every now and then I still read that letter
And get butterflies in my stomach.

Remember that small stuffed bear
You won for me at the fair?
It was a light brown color
With silly crooked eyes.
It still sits on my bed near my pillow
And stays there all night.

Remember the cd you made for me
When you were younger?
Some of the songs would skip around,
Or not play all the way through.
Every time I play that cd,
All I can think about is you.

Nostalgia is running through my veins,
Flashing images of you.
Such small and seemingly insignificant items
Mean more than anything.
The love we have
Is something I'll always remember.

Mosaic

Every time I meet a new person
Or find a new friend,
A small part of me comes from them.

Whether it's a silly phrase my best friends use
Or the way I tie my laces,
I have become a collage of other people.
When I met you, so many aspects changed.
I became a mosaic of you.
Every time I laugh, I sound a bit like you.

I find stupid jokes to be so funny.
I've learned to like new food,
And to try odd drinks.
So many pieces of me are like a mirror,
Reflecting who you are.
And with these small bits
Hidden within my very personality,
We become closer.
The light that shines between us guides
Our way through what we once
Considered to be dark.

Our eyes and lips meet in such perfect times,
While our hearts beat in synch.
Our history has merged into a book
Of battles and of peace.
We speak of the same dreams,
Passions, and wishes.

We have become a collection of art,
A perfect sculpture of marble.
We're something rather beautiful.

Soft Moments

What if we laid down in the middle of a field,
Full of green grass.
To feel the dirt on our arms,
To feel the sun on our skin.
We could forget the essence of time,
Forget about the troubles of the world.

We can pretend tomorrow doesn't exist.
It will simply be you and I together.
And as the sun sets,
Revealing pretty reds and oranges,
We'll stay right here while we wait for the stars.

It would be so easy to escape the
Forever-lasting reality we are forced to take part in.

We'll experience the deepest emotions,
Crying and laughing.
At some points, we may not say a thing.
We'll wonder about life, question one another.
We'll find peace among the chaos.

Even though we can't stay in this place forever,
The memory in itself will remain to be eternal
And that's what we'll hold onto.
We've suffered enough, love.
This here is our time.
This is the soft moment that we've been waiting for.

Forget Societal Ideals

To find a place, a moment, a state of being
That brings as much joy as this does
Is such a beautiful thing.

You and I holding hands, smelling fresh flowers,
Tanning under the sun.
So often do we precariously walk
On the edge of disaster,
Yet we find times like this.

We've never been ideal people,
We've never really fit in.
But for us to be able to have found one another
And feel like this, it truly may be a miracle.

On the brink of chaos, yet in a soothing mindset,
We conquer the tormenting
Thoughts of society.

There is no room here for daunting
Ideas of perfection,
Or the need to be certain people.
You and I are who we are,
And I wouldn't want it any other way.

Why try to be like others,
Why try to change our ways?
If we can find pleasure in the simplest of things,
Then we should try to do that forever.

I Love You

I had such a strong desire to communicate
How I felt about you,
Yet my desire to hide won.
I was never able to open up,
Look you in the eyes,
And tell you how I feel.

The love was in our kisses, our hugs,
It was in the time we spent together.
But I could never say it out loud.
I was afraid.
I was terrified, really.
So I began to write poems.
I could easily hide behind a pen and paper.

I could tell you how I felt without
Saying anything at all.
And that was enough for me.
And it was enough for you.
But I still had a fire burning within me,
Begging me to tell you those three words.

It was hard to do so.
Once before, when I had shared my
Deepest thoughts and emotions,
I was betrayed.
I swore to never make the same mistake.
But sitting here now, filling these pages
With ink, I find that maybe it isn't scary.

Maybe this time it's safe.
You have always been the one person
I felt this way about
Completely and thoroughly.
Well, my dear, I must now say,
I love you.

Take My Words

I once had only words for you,
With little else to offer.
I could give you a meaningful chat,
But I could not say that I loved you.

As I began to notice how you'd fade away,
I knew I needed to give something more.
For me to tell you about my view
Of the world was one thing.

But for me to make an attempt to show you
How much you meant was another.
Slowly, though, as you showed me affection,
I was able to give that back.

First I started to hold your hand,
Then I gave you a kiss.
From there my words became obsolete.
I didn't have to say a thing.

Instead, I could show you how much I cared.
I could show you what you meant to me.
Whether it was making you a meal,
Or simply lending an ear, I could finally offer more.

Accomplishing This

Out of all my accomplishments,
There is one that is my favorite.
It isn't fighting my own battles and winning.
It isn't helping others with their battles.

My favorite and most rewarding accomplishment
Was pulling you out of a dark place
And seeing you smile.
For so long had you shown only
A frown on your lips.

Your eyes were dull, your voice drawn out.
But when I saved you from losing yourself,
I was able to bring you to life
You smiled wide, your eyes started to shine.

Your voice sounded like a song.
We started to do things together,
Spend time in the same room.
You were willing to try new things.
You were able to laugh.

You finally found yourself in a world
That looks like a maze.

Thank You, Love

I once felt grief so strong
That it shattered my heart.
My chest was heavy with regret and agony.
My stomach was tied in knots so tight
That I thought it might break.

My eyes were glossed over with tears that never fell.
I was stuck in a place
So vast and so terrible.
Yet here I stand today,
With a light air filling my lungs
And happy tears running down my cheeks.
Despite how fragmented I was,
You were there to save me.

You would sit on the floor with me
At night while I rocked myself to sleep.
You held me in your arms every time
I'd fall down with anguish.
I begged you to leave me there,
To stop trying.

But you never did.
I felt so stupid to have such awful feelings.
I felt stupid when I finally let you in.
Yet letting you in was about the best
Possible thing I could have done.
You were the only person who

Cared enough to help me fight
What I was feeling.

My heart was finally mended,
My soul complete.
And for that I thank you.
And I will continue to thank you
Until the day I die
For I will forever be grateful.

To Fall In Love

To fall in love is something beautiful.
It can be scary, it can be terrifying.
But it can also be thrilling and exciting.
You have the ability to share your vulnerability
And fears with another person.

The world becomes brighter,
And you feel everything much stronger.
It's like you're on a roller coaster.
Your stomach is doing flips,
Your heart starts to beat faster.

You finally find someone that you
Share so much with.
They're the person you can't wait to see.
They're the person you go to when you feel sad.

They're the first person you share
Something exciting with.
Your person is the one you want to
Embrace after a long day.
It's magical and quite honestly
Indescribable in some cases,
As love will never be the same for everyone.

You get the desire to put your
Best effort forward.
At the end of it all,
You finally feel complete.

There will be struggles,
And you might not think you're doing things right.
But no matter what you go through,
The love you experience may very well
Be the best feeling in the entire world.

Because despite what you may
Face with a lover, you get to make a choice.
You can choose to walk away,
Or you can choose to love
Someone with every part of your being.